Some Babies Are Wild

story by **Marion Dane Bauer** *photography by* **Stan Tekiela**

Adventure Publications
Cambridge, Minnesota

Dedication

For Chester
    —Marion Dane Bauer

To my daughter Abby, who loves baby animals as much as I do.
May your love of nature grow with each passing year.
    —Stan Tekiela

Cover and book design by Jonathan Norberg

10 9 8

Copyright © 2008 by Marion Dane Bauer and Stan Tekiela
Published by Adventure Publications
An imprint of AdventureKEEN
310 Garfield Street South
Cambridge, Minnesota 55008
(800) 678-7006
www.adventurepublications.net
Printed in China
ISBN 978-1-59193-084-6 (pbk.); ISBN 978-1-59193-573-5 (ebook)

Some Babies Are

Wild

Some babies are soft.

Some babies are prickly.

Some babies are very slow

and some move quickly.

Some live underground.

Some live inside a tree.

Some live in a house
just like you and me.

Some babies awaken
with the first daylight.

Some of them are up
in the middle of the night.

Some babies like to climb.

Some like to cling.

Some hang on tight

and some take wing.

Some babies are light

and some are dark.

Some eat bright berries

and some munch on bark.

Most babies like to discover

one another.

But all babies love Mama.

And Mama loves baby, too.

Just as YOUR Mama

loves you!

Eastern Cottontail

Baby cottontails—known as kits—are born in shallow holes in the ground. These small nests (also called "forms") are lined with fur from the mother and are covered with leaves. Kits enter the world without fur and with their eyes closed. But as soon as they develop fur and have their eyes open, they leave the nest and mother to live on their own.

DID YOU KNOW?
One difference between a hare and a rabbit is that a hare turns white during winter, while a rabbit does not. The eastern cottontail is a rabbit.

North American Porcupine

A porcupine mother gives birth to just one baby per year. The porcupette is born with its eyes open and with all of its quills, which start out soft and flexible but will harden within hours of birth. Born in late spring, the baby is able to feed by itself within one week but stays with its mother until the first autumn.

DID YOU KNOW?
The baby porcupine must be careful when nursing or cuddling with Mom. Otherwise, they might get poked by her sharp quills.

Painted Turtle

A female painted turtle can lay up to twenty eggs, once or twice per year. The mother digs a hole with her back legs to deposit the eggs and lets the sun warm the underground nest. Her eggs take seventy to eighty days to hatch. Some young turtles (hatchlings) remain in the underground nest during winter and will dig out of it the following spring.

DID YOU KNOW?
The temperature of a nest determines whether male or female turtles will be born. If the nest is warm (around 85 degrees) then female turtles will be born. It is cooler (around 77 degrees) male turtles will hatch. If the temperature is in between, both male and female turtles will be born.

Cougar

Baby cougars (called kittens) are born helpless, with their eyes closed. They begin their lives covered in dark spots, but the spots begin to fade after three months and are gone within a year. Young cougars stay inside the den until they are fifty to seventy days old, and they stay with their mothers for about a year before going off on their own.

DID YOU KNOW?
Mother cougars have kittens just once every two years. That way, they can spend more time with their babies and teach them how to survive.

Coyote

Coyote pups are born with their eyes closed and are dependent upon their parents for food and shelter. They stay inside the den, wrestling with their brothers and sisters (usually three to five of them). Their parents hunt for food, bringing it back to the den for the pups to eat.

DID YOU KNOW?
A mother coyote must plan ahead before giving birth to her pups. She digs an underground den in the fall, before winter begins. Otherwise, the ground might still be frozen when it's time to have her babies in late winter.

Northern Raccoon

Native only to North and Central America, raccoons give birth during spring. A mother raccoon has three to six babies, who stay inside the den until they are seven or eight weeks old. A raccoon's den might be found in a tree, underground or inside a building or shelter, such as a barn.

DID YOU KNOW?
The raccoon's species name is *lotor*, which means "washer," because raccoons are known to occasionally wash their food before eating. Raccoons also use their skilled hands to open doors, coolers and latches.

Eastern Bluebird

A mother bluebird lays up to six light-blue eggs twice per year. The chicks begin to hatch about two weeks later. Bluebird chicks start their lives with only a few feathers on their heads and wings. However, their feathers grow quickly; in just fifteen or sixteen days the young begin to fly.

DID YOU KNOW?
Bluebirds help their moms. Sometimes, the first group (or "brood") of bluebirds born each year assists their mother in raising the second group.

American Goldfinch

Goldfinches start nesting during the middle or end of summer. They wait for the seeds of wild thistle plants to mature, so they have plenty of food for their growing babies. Goldfinch eggs hatch within two weeks, and the chicks begin flying with their parents about fifteen days later.

DID YOU KNOW?
Goldfinch chicks are different than most baby birds because they eat seeds. Most baby birds are fed insects.

Eastern Screech-Owl

The mother screech-owl lays her eggs in a tree cavity or nest box that is dry and warm. She lays four or five eggs, which hatch in less than a month. At first, the baby owlets are nearly helpless; they can only raise their heads to beg for food. But five or six days later, they are strong enough to feed themselves. At that time, their parents begin dropping food into the nest, which the owlets must catch and eat on their own.

DID YOU KNOW?
Screech-owls rarely screech. Their typical call sounds more like a trill or a high-pitched whistle.

Black Bear

Mother black bears usually have two cubs once every two years (though they can have up to five cubs at one time). The cubs are born in January or February, while their mother is still hibernating in her underground den. After the cubs are born, the mother remains awake to make sure her cubs are nursing and staying warm. She also licks the cubs to help them stay clean.

DID YOU KNOW?
Black bears aren't just black, they are often brown, red, or cinnamon, among other colors.

Virginia Opossum

Newborn opossums (joeys) are very tiny. They are about the size of a navy bean. At birth, joeys have no fur and their eyes are shut. But they still manage to crawl inside their mother's fur-lined pouch, where they stay for two months.

DID YOU KNOW?
Young opossums ride on their mother's back until they are too big to do so. By then, they will have pulled most of the fur off her back.

Wood Duck

Newly hatched ducklings remain in the nest with their mother for only one day. On the second day, the mother leaves the nest and calls to her ducklings. The chicks take turns jumping to the ground below. When all of the ducklings are out of the nest, their mother leads them into a nearby lake. The ducklings will never return to their nest.

DID YOU KNOW?
Several wood duck mothers often lay their eggs together in a single nest, resulting in up to thirty eggs per nest.

Domestic Chicken

Mother chickens, or hens, can lay one egg every twenty-five hours. If the egg is fertilized, the egg hatches and a chick is born about twenty-one days later. Chicks come in a variety of colors including yellow, black, brown and red. They are able to stand, walk and follow their mothers within hours of hatching.

DID YOU KNOW?
There are more chickens in the world than any other bird species. It is estimated that more than 24 billion chickens inhabit the earth at any given time.

American Beaver

A mother beaver gives birth to up to eight babies each year. These babies, known as kits, are born with fur and can swim underwater within one week. Beavers have special valves that close off their ears and nostrils for underwater swimming.

DID YOU KNOW?
Many people think beavers eat wood, but it isn't true. They use wood for their dams, but actually eat the soft bark of smaller tree branches.

White-tailed Deer

Young deer, known as fawns, are covered with light spots that look like dappled sunlight to help hide from predators. Predators have trouble smelling them too, as fawns don't give off an odor. Fawns can walk just hours after birth, but they will lie quietly all day waiting for their mother to come and feed them after dark.

DID YOU KNOW?
While most animals live in dens or nests, white-tailed deer do not have permanent homes. They sleep in a different spot almost every night.

Gray Wolf

Gray wolf pups are born just like puppy dogs. Their eyes are closed, and they are helpless. Baby wolves come in a variety of colors, but most are gray. Some wolves change colors as they age, becoming gray or silver, especially around the face, just like people.

DID YOU KNOW?
Wolves live in large family units called "packs." A pack of wolves works together to hunt for food. Young wolves will stay with their parents' pack until they are two to three years old.

About the Author

Marion Dane Bauer is the author of more than sixty books for young people, ranging from novelty and picture books through early readers, both fiction and nonfiction, books on writing, and middle-grade and young-adult novels. She has won numerous awards, including the Minnesota Book Award, a Jane Addams Peace Association Award for her novel *Rain of Fire* and an American Library Association Newbery Honor Award for another novel, *On My Honor*, and the Kerlan Award from the University of Minnesota for the body of her work. She is a writing teacher as well as a writer and was first Faculty Chair and continues on the faculty at Vermont College of Fine Arts for the first Master of Fine Arts in Writing for Children and Young Adults program in the country. Her writing book, the *American Library Association Notable What's Your Story? A Young Person's Guide to Writing Fiction*, is used by writers of all ages. Adults who are interested in writing for children have found it especially useful. Her books have been translated into more than a dozen different languages. Visit her website at www.mariondanebauer.com.

About the Photographer

Naturalist, wildlife photographer and writer Stan Tekiela is the author of the popular nature appreciation book series that includes *Cranes, Herons & Egrets.* He has authored more than 165 field guides, nature books, children's books, wildlife audio CDs, puzzles and playing cards, presenting many species of birds, mammals, reptiles, amphibians, trees, wildflowers and cacti in the United States.

With a Bachelor of Science degree in Natural History from the University of Minnesota and as an active professional naturalist for more than 25 years, Stan studies and photographs wildlife throughout the United States and Canada. He has received various national and regional awards for his books and photographs. Also a well-known columnist and radio personality, his syndicated column appears in more than 25 newspapers and his wildlife programs are broadcast on a number of Midwest radio stations. Stan can be followed on Facebook and Twitter. He can be contacted via www.naturesmart.com.

Get All of the Award-Winning Duo's Children's Books

If you enjoyed *Some Babies Are Wild* you'll love these other titles that pair Marion Dane Bauer's touching stories with Stan Tekiela's incredible photography:

Baby Bear Discovers the World

Follow along as Baby Bear ventures into the forest to meet other animals. This popular book won the 2007 Mom's Choice Award for Most Outstanding Children's Book.

Cutest Critter

Which is the cutest critter in all the land? Find out in this award winning picture book. Stan Tekiela's photographs will have readers of all ages "oohing" and "aahing," and Marion Dane Bauer's answer to the question, "Who's the cutest critter?" might surprise you.